THE PETITION

Dedicated to
Peggy Ashcroft,
who inspired it,
Hume Cronyn and Jessica Tandy,
who gave it its first breath,
and
Peter Hall,
who revealed it to us

BRIAN CLARK

THE PETITION

AMBER LANE PRESS

All rights whatsoever in this play are strictly reserved and
application for performance etc. should be made before
rehearsal to:
Judy Daish Associates Ltd.
83 Eastbourne Mews
London W2 6LQ
No performance may be given unless a licence has been
obtained.

First published in 1986 by
Amber Lane Press Ltd.
9 Middle Way
Oxford OX2 7LH

Distributed in the USA by
Applause Theatre Books
211 West 71 Street
New York, NY 10023

Typset in Baskerville by
Oxford Computer Typesetting Ltd.
Printed in Great Britain by
Cotswold Press Ltd., Oxford

Library of Congress Cataloguing-in-Publication Data
Clark, Brian.
   The Petition.
   I. Title.
PR6053.L292P4   1986   822′.914   86-1213
ISBN 0-87910-265-9

CHARACTERS

GENERAL SIR EDMUND MILNE, 80
LADY ELIZABETH MILNE, 72

The play takes place in the drawing room of an elegant but homely Belgravia apartment. There are various reminders of a lifetime's military career in foreign parts, particularly in India.

Note: In order to clarify meanings for an American audience minimal changes were made to this English text. These are indicated in the form of footnotes where they occur.

The first production of *The Petition* opened at the Wilbur Theatre, Boston on 27 March 1986 and transferred to The Golden Theatre, Broadway on 24 April 1986. It was produced by Robert Whitehead – Roger L. Stevens and the Shubert Organization and directed by Sir Peter Hall with the following cast:

GENERAL SIR EDMUND MILNE: .... Hume Cronyn
LADY ELIZABETH MILNE: .... Jessica Tandy

The Petition is scheduled to open at the National Theatre, London on 28 July 1986, produced by the National Theatre in association with Astramead Ltd. and Freeshooter Ltd., directed by Sir Peter Hall with the following cast:

GENERAL SIR EDMUND MILNE: ....Sir John Mills
LADY ELIZABETH MILNE: .... Rosemary Harris

ACT ONE

LADY ELIZABETH MILNE *is reading the 'Guardian',*
GENERAL SIR EDMUND MILNE *is reading the 'Times'.*

*Between them on a coffee table are set cups of coffee
and a coffee pot.*

EDMUND *grunts in disgust at an item of news.*
ELIZABETH *looks at him but does not comment. She goes
back to her paper.*

EDMUND: ...Disgraceful...

> [*Again,* ELIZABETH *looks at him but does not
> comment. She returns to her paper. Suddenly*
> EDMUND *puts down his paper irritably and
> walks towards the whisky decanter on the side-
> board.*]

ELIZABETH: You haven't finished your coffee, dear.

> [EDMUND *hesitates, looking back at the coffee.*]

Don't you think suicide by alcohol is just a little
excessive as a response to the miners or the
Greenham Common women* — or whatever it
is that's upset you?

> [EDMUND *walks back to his chair and picks up
> his coffee.* ELIZABETH *smiles at him and returns
> to her paper.* EDMUND *looks at her. She is
> engrossed in her paper. She moves to ease a pain
> in her side.*]

EDMUND: Are you all right?

ELIZABETH: Yes thank you...

---

*U.S. text: ...as a response to the news — ...

[*She smiles and returns to her paper.* EDMUND *picks up his paper again. The same page causes him to grunt again.*]

EDMUND: Silly bugger!

ELIZABETH: Try the crossword, dear...

[EDMUND *looks at her, then folds the newspaper to the crossword.*]

EDMUND: What on earth can this mean...! "Music for the pensioner; what a bind!"

ELIZABETH: Bandage... Band... age...

EDMUND: ...Oh...!

[*He puts down the paper again.*]

You have to have a twisted mind to do the *Times'* crossword...

ELIZABETH: Yes, it does help...

[EDMUND *walks determinedly to the whisky and pours himself a whisky and water.*]

Edmund, you know the doctor said you should restrict yourself to just one before lunch.

EDMUND: It *is* before lunch...

ELIZABETH: It's ten o'clock.

EDMUND: ...I'll make it last.

[*He takes an exaggeratedly small sip and returns to his chair. He picks up the paper again and returns to the page that has annoyed him.*]

EDMUND: Incredible!

[ELIZABETH *resignedly puts down her paper.*]

ELIZABETH: You'd better get it off your chest.

EDMUND: I   pay...what?...twenty-five   pence   for   this paper...that's five shillings in real money...and one whole page is a petition, a list of all the reds, queers, out-of-work thespians, crooked politicians, do-gooders — all the out and out lunatics in the entire country.

ELIZABETH: Seems good value. You'll know who to avoid.

EDMUND: And the top of the whole list is Field Marshall Sir Jeremy Philips...

ELIZABETH: Jerry!

EDMUND: Leading the list of those faint-hearts who want to get rid of the bomb!

> [ELIZABETH *gets up and moves to* EDMUND. *She looks over his shoulder.*]

There you are...Look!

> [ELIZABETH *quickly runs her eye down the page. She moves away.*]

ELIZABETH: It's not a petition to ban the bomb, dear. Just to renounce the first use of it.

EDMUND: What the hell's the use of having the thing if you advertise to the enemy that you're not going to use it?

ELIZABETH: Not going to use it *first*.

EDMUND: So he can shell you, bomb you, nerve gas you, burn you with napalm, kill you with anthrax and you promise just to use catapults.

ELIZABETH: Don't we have shells and tanks and things...?

EDMUND: Not as many as he has...and Jerry Philips *knows* that...I've always had my doubts about him ...Do you remember that bother in Bengal in...'35?

ELIZABETH: Oh Edmund. Everyone said how well he handled it, with minimum loss of life...

EDMUND: Yes. At the time. But it broke out again didn't it...? In '36. If he'd been firmer the year before, given them a lesson, then old Quinters wouldn't have had such a terrible job to do the next year.

ELIZABETH: I seem to remember "Old Quinters" enjoying it.

EDMUND: He was a good soldier...He'd have known how to cope with those Greenham Common women!*

ELIZABETH: Yes...you're right...he would have enjoyed firing into a bunch of unarmed women. It would have seemed to him just an extension of his marriage.

EDMUND: He never used violence on his wife!

ELIZABETH: No, but unlike those Bengalis, *she* never demanded to be treated as a human being!

EDMUND: And your idea of humanity is rioting in the streets, hurling stones at British soldiers, is it?

ELIZABETH: ...In some circumstances I suppose it is...

EDMUND: Well, it isn't mine.

ELIZABETH: No, I know. Stones are far too inaccurate...

[EDMUND *dismisses this with a grunt.*]

Edmund, why are you defending Jack Quinley? You know as well as I do how his treatment of his wife in public used to embarrass you.

EDMUND: ...Well...he may not have been as sensitive to a woman's feelings as he might have been — but he was a good soldier for all that.

ELIZABETH: And Jerry wasn't?

EDMUND: I'm not saying that. In war he was good — damned good, but as an aid to the civil power, I had my doubts.

[*He strikes the paper.*]

This proves it. What can he have been thinking about to lead this lot into battle? He must have become senile.

ELIZABETH: He hasn't.

---

*U.S. text: ...those Ban-the Bomb women!

EDMUND: I mean look at them...Dame Edna Fairly, an actress! What the hell does she know about nuclear strategy?

ELIZABETH: What we all know.

EDMUND: Sir Kenneth Canning — a painter, Jasper Delton, an architect, Phillipa Hughes, a novelist ...Neil Kinnock...Ken Livingstone...Helen M —

[*He stops and looks harder at the page.*]
...Lady Elizabeth Milne...
[*He looks at his wife.*]
...Lady Elizabeth Milne...You!

ELIZABETH: That's right. One of London's more celebrated lunatics.

EDMUND: You gave them permission to...to put your name...?

ELIZABETH: I signed the petition...

EDMUND: But why?

ELIZABETH: I believed in it.

EDMUND: ...You can't have.

ELIZABETH: Why not?

EDMUND: It doesn't make sense.

ELIZABETH: It does to me.

EDMUND: ...You've *never* taken a public stand on anything!

ELIZABETH: Perhaps it's time to start!

[EDMUND *drops the paper on the chair. He picks up his whisky, drinks and walks to the window.*]

EDMUND: ...Did it occur to you how it would...humiliate *me*?

ELIZABETH: ...When I signed it, I wasn't thinking of you. But of course I knew you wouldn't be pleased.

EDMUND: How could you do it, Elizabeth?

ELIZABETH: Because I felt strongly about it.

EDMUND: You could have talked to me.

ELIZABETH: I learned many years ago not to talk politics with you.

EDMUND: ...I can't understand it!

ELIZABETH: No.

EDMUND: What is that supposed to mean!

ELIZABETH: Just what I said. I understand you can't understand it.

EDMUND: Because you think I'm stupid?

ELIZABETH: No! Of course not. It's just that you think within strictly defined limits.

EDMUND: You mean I'm limited?

ELIZABETH: No. You limit yourself. Deliberately. As a matter of...of policy...philosophy even. In fact, of course, you are very intelligent with a clear logical mind.

EDMUND: Thank you.

ELIZABETH: So, having laid down the ground rules of your life, all your beliefs, actions can be predicted.

EDMUND: How boring for you.

ELIZABETH: To be honest, I *have* sometimes thought so, but on many, many more occasions I have realised it also means I can count on you — and I have appreciated that.

[*She returns to her chair. She looks at* EDMUND *still suffering by the window.*]

I'm sorry, Edmund...Not sorry to have signed it, but I'm sorry to have caused you pain...

EDMUND: ...What did you expect?

ELIZABETH: ...Well...I suppose I expected you to be extremely angry and to flounce off down to your club.

EDMUND: I'm glad I still have power to surprise you.

ELIZABETH: ...Yes...so am I.

EDMUND: As for going down to the club...you've made that rather difficult, don't you think?

ELIZABETH: Because of your friends...They'll laugh at you...

EDMUND: They're probably sniggering already.

ELIZABETH: Yes.

EDMUND: ...I didn't know you were involved with those people.

ELIZABETH: Involved is...is too strong a word...I've sent them a small donation from time to time...

EDMUND: A donation? I didn't know anything about that!

ELIZABETH: It was from my personal account. You've never kept me informed about how you spend your own money — and nor should you have.

EDMUND: Nevertheless! To send money to...

ELIZABETH: Is "traitors" the word you're looking for?

EDMUND: They're not far short. Why couldn't you send your money to Famine Relief or something...?

ELIZABETH: So the condemned man can eat a hearty breakfast!

EDMUND: It's not funny, Elizabeth! You're exposing us to ridicule.

ELIZABETH: I think that's going a bit far...If husbands and wives who have different opinions are ridiculous, we are members of a very large club.

EDMUND: It's not the difference of opinion that matters, it's the exposing of it to every Tom, Dick and Harry.

ELIZABETH: Ah, I see! Not in front of the children.

EDMUND: Precisely. We are privileged to lead in some small way and it is therefore our duty to support the Sovereign and her Government whatever our private opinions.

ELIZABETH: But you are retired, Edmund. You are eighty

for God's sake! You're not in the army any more!

EDMUND: Officers do not retire. They merely go on half pay. I still hold the Queen's Commission and shall do until the day I die.

ELIZABETH: So does Jerry, presumably, but he doesn't believe that makes him a political eunuch.

EDMUND: Jerry!

ELIZABETH: As a matter of fact, his signing it encouraged me enormously.

EDMUND: Did you know that he was going to sign it...?

ELIZABETH: Yes I did, as a matter of fact.

EDMUND: Did he ask you to sign it?

ELIZABETH: No...If you want to know, I asked him.

EDMUND: When...?

ELIZABETH: About a fortnight ago.

EDMUND: But we haven't seen him for months.

ELIZABETH: *You* haven't seen him for months.

EDMUND: But you haven't been out...not since your illness...he...he came here...?

ELIZABETH: Yes...he came to see me when I was in hospital a year ago. Since then he's come round every Wednesday for tea...

EDMUND: Oh my God...Why didn't you tell me?

ELIZABETH: I didn't think it would increase the pleasure of your bridge afternoon.

EDMUND: It's so underhand...I'm not surprised at Jerry, but you...

ELIZABETH: What about me? Surely you don't suspect we've been having a geriatric love affair? What with Jerry's tin leg and my "women's insides", as you delicately refer to them, any attempt at coition would be more likely to end in extreme embarrassment than orgasm.

EDMUND: I didn't mean that.

ELIZABETH: Didn't you? You've never liked Jerry...ever since Calcutta in '33...You've always wondered if we had an affair then.

EDMUND: And did you...? No, there's no need to answer that...I don't want ...

ELIZABETH: No...we didn't...Jerry was — and is — too much of a gentleman.

EDMUND: I would have preferred it if you'd said you were too much of a lady.

ELIZABETH: But we both know that isn't true.

EDMUND: I don't know that...

[ELIZABETH *smiles at him.*]

ELIZABETH: I suppose lack of imagination is an asset to a soldier. If you could imagine all those guns pointing, it would be much more difficult to charge them.

EDMUND: It's also an asset to a pacifist. If you can't imagine what it would be like living under the Russian jackboot, it is much easier to disarm yourself.

ELIZABETH: Oh, I can imagine that all right; I'd rather be dead. Believe me, Edmund, if Ivan lands at Dover even I would urge you to charge him and if my "women's insides" will let me, I'll be by your side.

EDMUND: So what's that nonsense about...?

[*He waves at the paper.*]

ELIZABETH: That's different.

EDMUND: It isn't. The bomb is to deter Ivan from contemplating landing at Dover.

ELIZABETH: Just as the Maginot Line was supposed to deter Hitler?

EDMUND: That was a complete cock-up.

ELIZABETH: And you believe that that was the very last cock that the world's armies will up?

EDMUND: On that scale, yes...The alternative is too horrible.

ELIZABETH: It was thinking about Hitler which made up my mind about the bomb. I'm glad the French didn't have it to throw when Adolf burst through the Maginot line.

EDMUND: Around it. It should have extended to the North Sea.

ELIZABETH: They had a rough five years but they were liberated in the end. And now French children are still being born with only one head.

EDMUND: Believe me. The Russian rule of Britain would last for a hell of a lot longer than five years.

ELIZABETH: So? If it comes to that, I'm glad King Harold of England didn't have it to lob at William the Conqueror, or the Celts at the Romans who destroyed our way of life for three hundred years. I'm glad the Nicaraguans don't have it to throw at the Americans. Empires come and empires go; it would be good to think the planet could go on forever. At least 'til God snuffs out the sun.

EDMUND: But if we have the bomb it won't happen.

ELIZABETH: If we have the bomb it *will*. You're the sort of chap who would have put money on Hitler's sanity.

EDMUND: He was as mad as a hatter but not so mad that he would have risked a war with England if he'd believed we would fight; *known* we would die rather than let him put one foot on Polish soil.

ELIZABETH: Being willing to die for your country is a decent, honourable feeling. Being willing to wipe out the planet because you and your children can't rule a bit of it for a few hundred years is a monstrous arrogance.

> [*A pain catches her in the side again. She holds herself and sinks back into her chair.*]

EDMUND: Steady, Liz old girl...insides again?

ELIZABETH: ...Oh Edmund! You're a funny old stick. You've waded through the blood of your own men on the battlefield, but concerning my late lamented uterus, you're as squeamish as a little boy.

EDMUND: Can I get you something...? One of your pills...?

ELIZABETH: Yes...they're on the sideboard...

> [EDMUND *hurries over to the sideboard. He takes a pill out of the box.*]

EDMUND: Some water?

> [ELIZABETH *nods.* EDMUND *pours some water.*]

ELIZABETH: As you've decided the sun is over the yardarm or whatever, perhaps you'd flavour it a little with some of your brown medicine there.

> [EDMUND *looks at her, realises, smiles and adds some whisky to the water. He brings it to her. She takes the pill and a sip of whisky.*]

EDMUND: I've never seen you drink in the morning.

ELIZABETH: You won't report me to Alcoholics Anonymous?

EDMUND: No...I've no intention of going there...I'm not an alcoholic.

ELIZABETH: That's better.

EDMUND: Should I get the quack in?

ELIZABETH: No...no need...

[*The pain recedes. So does* EDMUND.]

EDMUND: You're right of course. We shouldn't talk politics. We've never agreed. Especially when you're not yourself.

ELIZABETH: We've agreed even less when I *am* myself...

EDMUND: You know what I mean.

ELIZABETH: You've never forgiven me for voting Labour in 1945, have you?

EDMUND: To be quite honest with you Elizabeth, I never really believed you did.

ELIZABETH: Well I'm damned! You think I was just teasing you?

EDMUND: Well...yes!

ELIZABETH: Very well, General Sir Edmund Milne, let me tell you this — I didn't before because after '45 it didn't seem worth the candle. But I have voted Labour in *every* election *since* 1945.

EDMUND: I don't believe it.

ELIZABETH: I did.

EDMUND: Even for that red Michael Foot?

ELIZABETH: Yes!

EDMUND: Now I *know* you're not telling the truth.

ELIZABETH: I can see I should have always told the truth about everything. If it was unpleasant you wouldn't have believed it.

EDMUND: You mean you haven't always told me the truth?

ELIZABETH: Well...you know...

EDMUND: What have you lied to me about...?

ELIZABETH: Nothing specific...I was joking...

EDMUND: Were you?

[ELIZABETH *looks at him a long time.*]

ELIZABETH: ...If you're playing a game, Edmund, be careful. It's dangerous.

EDMUND: Who's playing a game?

ELIZABETH: ...Very well...The truth...Where shall we start...? Money...? Sex...?

EDMUND: What are you talking about...?

ELIZABETH: You asked me what I'd lied about...so I'm prepared to think back and try to remember all the times I've been less than strictly honest. I suppose we could start with the little things, like the times when I've been overdrawn in the bank without telling you and the odd faked orgasm and then move on to more serious things, like...

EDMUND: This is ridiculous.

ELIZABETH: You don't want me to go on?

EDMUND: I don't want to quarrel with you, Elizabeth.

ELIZABETH: No... [*She relaxes and smiles.*] That's been our tragedy.

EDMUND: Tragedy! You would have preferred us to have conducted our lives like Billingsgate fishwives?

[ELIZABETH *considers the proposition.*]

ELIZABETH: Sounds lively, anyway.

EDMUND: I wish you'd take me seriously.

ELIZABETH: ...Honestly, Edmund...I can't think what to say to that. *You* wish *I'd* take *you* seriously?

EDMUND: That's exactly what I said.

ELIZABETH: Yes. I heard. Did you hear me saying exactly the same thing about me all morning?

EDMUND: You mean about that...that petition thing...?

ELIZABETH: Yes...I didn't sign it on a whim. It wasn't a piece of childish rebellion, or pique, or seeking notoriety. I thought about it carefully. I weighed the arguments. All the pros and cons and finally, deliberately, when I decided I really believed in the proposition, I signed it. And I beg you to take that seriously.

EDMUND: You felt that strongly?

ELIZABETH: I did!

EDMUND: ...Then I have to accept it.

ELIZABETH: Thank you, Edmund. I mean it, thank you.

EDMUND: I accept you felt that strongly, but I don't understand it, or see why you had to make a public spectacle of us.

ELIZABETH: That's the nature of battles, Edmund. They can't be private. If you attack the enemy so gently and quietly that even he doesn't know he's being attacked, you're not likely to win.

EDMUND: And who's your enemy? Me?

ELIZABETH: Not you personally. But your opinions, your aggressiveness and — I have to say it — your arrogance, yes, in so far as you are your opinions, you are the enemy.

EDMUND: That's how you regard me?

ELIZABETH: No, of course I don't. It isn't as simple as that.

EDMUND: It seems that way to me.

ELIZABETH: Then you're not being honest.

EDMUND: So you can add habitual liar to your list of my charming attributes.

ELIZABETH: Stop being so childish, Edmund. Why is it you regard fighting a battle in war as so complex and human relationships as so simple? It's the other way round.

EDMUND: You've never tried organising a division with all its supplies to deliver a decisive punch — and keep the whole thing secret.

ELIZABETH: But I have lived with you for fifty odd years...! Oh! That was a cheap crack... But you do regard human relationships as simple and they're not! You can analyse a battle fairly easily. Try analysing one human personality, never mind a relationship.

EDMUND: I've never gone along with all that psychoanalysis nonsense. It's just a way of people finding reasons for not doing what they ought to do.

ELIZABETH: Then you refuse to use a powerful tool for trying to understand people. You'd rather see them as some sort of automata running along a railway track — or falling off it — rather than a whole wonderful, mysterious collection of drives and impulses, hopes and fears, mind and body, that moves God knows where, God knows why.

EDMUND: Of course I don't see people as robots. It's *because* I see the difficulties that I know you have to choose some pretty simple rules to live by — and stick to them, not cop out when the going gets rough.

ELIZABETH: And what if the rules are leading to chaos? It's madness to follow them to self-destruction.

EDMUND: If you think I'm mad, I can see why it wasn't so hard to have our name printed in association with that harum-scarum lot.

ELIZABETH: I'm sorry it's *our* name. I can't be held responsible for that. I would have been perfectly happy to have kept my maiden name if I'd known I was going to bring shame on yours.

EDMUND: Perhaps you wish you had kept your maiden name in any case...not married me...

ELIZABETH: Do you really want to discuss that?

EDMUND: ...No...I've done what I can...always...you've

always been number one for me...I'm sorry
...if...if you don't feel the same way.

ELIZABETH: Edmund...It's hard to believe marriages are
made in heaven. But wherever ours was made,
we're still here...together...and we have four
fine children to leave after us and seven grandchildren and in a month our first great grand-
child.

EDMUND: Yes, the bloody fool. Fancy getting her pregnant. He's only twenty.

ELIZABETH: Were you a virgin at twenty?

EDMUND: Of course not. I was at Sandhurst.

ELIZABETH: Well, I can't think it's worse to get carried
away with a girl you're in love with — and
standing by her — than banging away at a
West End prostitute without giving a damn for
her — or for yourself for that matter.

EDMUND: We were just young men...no harm in it.

ELIZABETH: Maybe. But it seems to me that lots of young
people nowadays are older than we've ever
been.

EDMUND: Nonsense!

ELIZABETH: Think, Edmund...The thirties in Calcutta. Did
it seem it would ever end? The mess nights,
dinners at the club, polo on the Maidan. Stacks
of deferential servants. Do you remember the
Regent's ball in the Vice-Regal Lodge? That
wonderful room all white and gold with the
band in the gallery...the girls in their new ball-
gowns, the men in their number one kit — gold
braid and shiny buttons. It was a dream land.
A fairy tale. Did I tell you that Nancy went
back to Calcutta last year?

EDMUND: No.

ELIZABETH: She did. Just for a holiday. A tour. To see the old places. The Vice-Regal Lodge is now the National Library. The paint is peeling. Some of the fans don't work — and in any case they have six hours of power cuts most days.

EDMUND: I'm not at all surprised.

ELIZABETH: The girls in their white dresses and shining young men have gone, but it's still full of young people studying agriculture, engineering, medicine, literature. To hell with the white dresses, I say. Libraries before ballrooms.

EDMUND: At least they have a building they can *use* as a library.

ELIZABETH: To listen to you, you'd think the Indians were savages before us...They did build before the big white sahib showed them how to lay brick on brick. The Taj Mahal was built before we got there!

[EDMUND *moves to the sideboard carrying his empty glass.*]

Edmund, please don't drink any more this morning...You never used to...It's very recent ...And you get so bad-tempered when you have one too many.

EDMUND: What the hell do you mean!

[ELIZABETH *smiles at him.*]

All right, all right.

[*He puts down his empty glass and paces.*]

ELIZABETH: Come and sit down...Please...This isn't a barrack square and it's very hard to talk to you if you're on the move all the time.

EDMUND: That's the idea. It's harder to hit a moving target.

ELIZABETH: Please!

[EDMUND *stops pacing, looks at her and reluctantly resumes his seat.*]

I'm sorry about Jerry. Not telling you. I suppose if I told the truth I'd have to admit I enjoyed it rather...like an intrigue. Not that it was...I don't know why I feel so foolish, protesting my innocence at my age...

EDMUND: I don't know why either...I still find you attractive...desirable.

ELIZABETH: Thank you.

EDMUND: Even if your insides...er...

ELIZABETH: Aren't able to be so hospitable as formerly? I'm sorry, Edmund, really I am...

EDMUND: Don't be silly...The only thing that matters is that you get well again. Get rid of that damned stitch that keeps catching you.

ELIZABETH: Yes...but I wouldn't mind if you found it necessary to...well, to find someone else occasionally.

EDMUND: Oh, Elizabeth...what do you think I am? Some young stud that has to have his oats regularly? In any case, where would I find somebody else?

ELIZABETH: So you have thought of it.

EDMUND: Of course I haven't...I was just saying...even if I did where would I...?

ELIZABETH: Well...when you were in Sandhurst...

EDMUND: I have no desire to go banging away, as you put it, at a West End prostitute...especially after you.

ELIZABETH: Thank you...I can't remember when you've said anything so nice to me. Not for ages.

EDMUND: Women! Say you prefer your wife to a prostitute and they come over all unnecessary.

ELIZABETH: There's something else I have to say. Not telling you was my idea. Not Jerry's. He wasn't very happy about it. But I insisted. I knew you'd feel you had to stay, be a host, all that. And it wasn't necessary. Especially as you and Jerry have never been...well...close...So don't be angry with him will you? Feel it necessary to call him out at dawn?

EDMUND: All right. But I reserve the right to be bloody angry with him for signing that petition, bringing the whole army into disrepute. Conduct unbecoming. I shall sort him out about that...even if I am at the back of a long queue.

ELIZABETH: Well, that's up to you.

EDMUND: Did you really ask him?

ELIZABETH: Yes.

EDMUND: Did you have to persuade him?

ELIZABETH: On the contrary. I showed him the petition, he read it, took out his pen and signed it.

EDMUND: Weren't you surprised?

ELIZABETH: No...We'd done a lot of talking over the year. I would have been surprised if he hadn't signed.

[EDMUND *shakes his head in disbelief.*]

EDMUND: Makes a nonsense of his whole life.

ELIZABETH: He doesn't think so. He isn't a pacifist. His whole life has been dedicated to keeping order with the minimum force necessary. For him, reducing the planet to an uninhabited heap of frozen radioactive ash does not constitute keeping order.

EDMUND: ...Well...I probably shan't see him. He doesn't go to the club much anyway and after this I doubt he'll go again. So even if I decide to go...

ELIZABETH: Of course you'll go. It's your life, Edmund.

EDMUND: You have to see...after this...

ELIZABETH: I'm damned if I see. I'm not an appendage of *you*. I have my own life, my own decisions. You're not responsible for me!

EDMUND: It's not so simple.

ELIZABETH: It is so simple. If any of them get on to you, tell them if they'd been man enough to marry someone who was their own woman, not some droopy dependent creature, they'd have the right to criticise. But if they had, of course they wouldn't want to.

EDMUND: You've always been so...powerful, Elizabeth.

ELIZABETH: Too powerful?

EDMUND: ...No...

ELIZABETH: That didn't sound very convincing.

EDMUND: Well...it hasn't been easy, has it...?

ELIZABETH: No...not for either of us. Do you know what the hardest part for me was?

EDMUND: What?

ELIZABETH: The war.

EDMUND: Of course! You were alone...for years.

ELIZABETH: It wasn't that...It was the knowledge that those were the happiest days of your life. You were fighting, often hungry, mostly bored, I expect; you watched friends die and become horribly maimed. In spite of all that, it was better than ...than living with me.

EDMUND: I'm a soldier, Liz old girl...

ELIZABETH: Yes.

EDMUND: It was what I had been preparing for, all my life before then.

ELIZABETH: Yes. I understand. But it's hard.

EDMUND: You did a marvellous job in the war. Keeping

the family together, working in the War House
...you did your bit...

ELIZABETH: Oh, I read a funny story about the War Office
the other day. Evidently a messenger couldn't
find it in Whitehall so he stopped a soldier to
ask which side it was on. The soldier hesitated
and said, "Well, I'm not sure, but I *think* it's on
ours."

> [EDMUND *laughs.*]

EDMUND: I know how that soldier felt...yes...those were
the days...sorry!

> [ELIZABETH *smiles.* EDMUND *makes his way to
> the window.* ELIZABETH *picks up her 'Guar-
> dian' again.*]

I'd better ring James this morning.

ELIZABETH: Oh...? Why...?

EDMUND: Well...I don't know how long it takes the *Times*
to get to Brussels, but as you've taken a hand in
planning N.A.T.O. strategy, I daresay N.A.T.O.
H.Q. will get wind of it pretty quickly.

ELIZABETH: There's no hurry. It will take military intelli-
gence at least a month to uncover my threat to
the national security.

EDMUND: It's only fair to warn him.

ELIZABETH: I never thought of James.

EDMUND: Would it have made any difference?

ELIZABETH: No.

EDMUND: ...He'll take some ragging in the mess.

ELIZABETH: That doesn't matter, does it?

EDMUND: We're an Army family, Elizabeth.

ELIZABETH: Not all of us.

EDMUND: Even Simon's doctoral thesis was on the Trojan
War.

ELIZABETH: I think he was more interested in Homer's language than the details of military history.

EDMUND: I remember we talked a lot about it at the time.

ELIZABETH: ...Yes...He was very clever.

EDMUND: Clever? You mean he was humouring me?

ELIZABETH: No! He just met you on your ground. You wouldn't have wanted to talk about Homer's metrical structure would you...? I'm sure you helped him a lot.

EDMUND: The principles of war never change. The Greeks, Romans, Clausewitz. Always the same. Muster sufficient force to make a breakthrough, then have enough reserves to exploit it... Whether it's ten men in a wooden horse or every artillery piece Monty could lay his hands on at El Alamein. Punch a hole and pour through it. The principles never change.

ELIZABETH: Until now. Now you punch a hole, then before you can "pour through" you yourself die from the after-effects of the punch — and you take the planet with you.

EDMUND: We can't get away from it, can we?

ELIZABETH: No...I haven't been able to for months.

EDMUND: What brought it on?

ELIZABETH: You make it sound like the 'flu.

EDMUND: Something must have set you off...I know you. Once you get a bee in your bonnet you're like a terrier with a rat.

ELIZABETH: Bees, terriers, rats — a menagerie of mixed metaphor...sorry...What "brought it on?" Well ...I've always been interested in politics...You know that.

EDMUND: Indeed I know that...Sometimes I wondered if

I'd make a Colonel never mind General.

ELIZABETH: Oh, Edmund! I always thought about your career. I never once crossed the line.

EDMUND: Crossed it! You walked it like a tight-rope artist. I was always waiting for you to fall on the wrong side.

ELIZABETH: But I never did, did I? Not 'til now. And surely at the age of eighty you've given up hope of your baton.

EDMUND: You had some close calls...

ELIZABETH: Yes! It was fun! Do you remember Cowlishaw!

EDMUND: Do I remember Cowlishaw!

ELIZABETH: [*in a fruity military voice*] "Madam, are you implying that the Raj is bad for India?"

EDMUND: [*in a feminine voice*] "Oh, Colonel! With soldiers like you to guide her, I'm sure India will bear the mark of British rule for centuries."

ELIZABETH: Oh Edmund, you've remembered! How sweet of you!

EDMUND: If Cowlishaw hadn't been so stupid, he would have known what you meant. He was the only one in the mess who didn't. We were damned lucky.

ELIZABETH: I wasn't lucky. I knew him. He was so vain that provided a woman smiled at him she could say anything she liked. He was convinced that she had only one thought in her head and that was to see him without those preposterous jodhpurs he always wore.

EDMUND: You did take risks, though.

ELIZABETH: Edmund. I had to stay *alive*.

EDMUND: You haven't said what finally caused you to make a public spectacle of us.

ELIZABETH: ...Well, as I said, I was interested in politics and when I took that Open University degree ten years ago...

EDMUND: Ah, that's it!

ELIZABETH: What do you mean, "That's it"...? You were proud of me!

EDMUND: Well yes, I was, in a way. Though why a woman of over sixty should want to go back to school defeated me.

ELIZABETH: You were always going back to school. All through your career. Field Officers' Courses, Staff College, Senior Staff College.

EDMUND: But not after I retired...er...went on half pay.

ELIZABETH: Well, I haven't retired. Unfortunately I didn't have anything to retire from.

EDMUND: When *we* retired. From the Army.

ELIZABETH: Yes...but actually, Edmund, I retired from the Army a very long time ago. At the age of nineteen I didn't realise I was taking the King's shilling. I thought I was just marrying you. It didn't take me long to find out how much he wanted for his shilling, so privately, in my heart, I gave it back to him.

EDMUND: The only way you could do that was to leave me...Did you think of it?

ELIZABETH: Yes, I did...but...James was on the way.

EDMUND: You mean...if you hadn't have been pregnant, you would have left me?

ELIZABETH: No...It's too easy, that. I meant being pregnant I didn't really consider it. And if I had, no doubt I would have come up with all sorts of other reasons why I shouldn't leave you.

EDMUND: Oh well, that's very gratifying. Knowing that you were capable of finding all sorts of reasons

why we should stay married. Apart, that is,
from the boringly obvious ones...like...you
loved me. At least I thought you did.

ELIZABETH: I did...I do still as a matter of fact...but it was a
shock, Edmund, as a young wife of what, nine-
teen, twenty, to discover I was not just married
to you...but to an army, an empire.

EDMUND: You exaggerate!

ELIZABETH: No...! You remember the Victorian mother's
advice to her daughter on her wedding night.
"It won't be pleasant, dear, but just lie back
and think of England." Well, for me our love-
making was so marvellous because those were
the only times I *didn't* have to think about
bloody England.

EDMUND: But damn it all, Elizabeth. You knew the score.
You were *born* in India, you must have known.

ELIZABETH: But we weren't military. We were civil.

EDMUND: And was that so different?

ELIZABETH: ...No...I don't suppose it was really...Looking
back I suppose Mother married the Civil Ser-
vice just as I married the Army. That's what I
said just now. The young are so much wiser
than we were. Young girls nowadays don't behave as stupidly as I did.

EDMUND: I'm sorry if you think marrying me was stupid.

ELIZABETH: I didn't mean that and you know I didn't. Look
at Jane, for example. She didn't marry before
she graduated. Realised herself. Became her
own woman. Not like me. I really looked for-
ward to losing my virginity; I didn't know it
entailed losing my identity...before I'd even
found it.

EDMUND: A fat lot of good it did Jane.

ELIZABETH: I can't believe her marriage ended because she knew who she was. But whatever the reason she can support herself and her children.

EDMUND: The question is if she hadn't tried to carry on being a teacher and raising a family and looking after her husband, would the marriage have broken up in the first place?

ELIZABETH: You would deprive girls of an education just so they have no alternative but to stick to their husbands no matter how unhappy they are?

EDMUND: No, of course not...

ELIZABETH: Well, my education, my formal education came late but I'm glad it came some time. It was wonderful.

EDMUND: I was glad when it was over. Forever stuck in your books. Coming to bed at 1.30 after the TV lectures. Up at six to hear another on the radio. Summer schools...

ELIZABETH: It's sad, isn't it? Your best years were spent away from me — and my best years were spent away from you.

EDMUND: ...So...six years after you graduate, the full fruits of all that insomniac effort bursts forth in the *Times*. It was Harold Wilson that started the Open University, you know.

ELIZABETH: I know. But you mustn't blame him. My name's in the *Times*. His isn't. As far as I know he'll be perfectly happy to blast off with H-bombs when the first Russian scout car comes through the wire.

EDMUND: There you are, you see? There's no question of blasting off with H-bombs. Tactical warheads. Nuclear artillery. Pinpointed on military targets and supply lines.

ELIZABETH: Pinpointed! I like that. Some pin. Some pin-
hole. And do you think it would stop there? It
would be bound to escalate.
[*She feels her side again.*]

EDMUND: All right?

ELIZABETH: Yes...just a twinge.

EDMUND: We should stop this...It can't be doing you any
good.

ELIZABETH: But I haven't told you yet why I signed the
petition.

EDMUND: You said the degree and all that made you...

ELIZABETH: No...it was wonderful. Important to me. I'm
very grateful, Edmund, for your support in
that...

EDMUND: It was nothing.

ELIZABETH: I think it was something...it did clarify things
for me. Made it easier to think. To explain
things to myself. But I think I would have
signed that petition even if Harold Wilson had
never needed that idea for an election speech.
And in any case, it may have been Wilson who
thought of it, but it was Jennie Lee who made it
a reality. We have to thank a woman for that!

EDMUND: Hm!

ELIZABETH: Of course, that probably confirms your belief
that the whole thing was a mistake anyway.

EDMUND: Good God, woman! You're treating me like
some sort of caricature! I've never been against
women's rights.

ELIZABETH: No.

EDMUND: Or denied they've made an enormous contribu-
tion.

ELIZABETH: Mainly by providing sons to become soldiers.

EDMUND: No! Any soldier, for example, who has survived

a gunshot wound knows he probably owes his
life to Florence Nightingale.

ELIZABETH: Yes, that's all very well, Edmund, but women
can do other things than become sort of honor-
ary soldiers — "doing their bit in the War
House" or even in a field hospital.

EDMUND: Let's not go on. You're not addressing me, but
some figment of your imagination.

ELIZABETH: But I haven't told you why I signed the petition.

[*She holds her side.*]

EDMUND: There's no need to go on...take it easy.

ELIZABETH: It was in hospital a year ago. And for the first
time, I was really facing my death.

EDMUND: Please!

ELIZABETH: And I realised a strange thing. I didn't really
mind. Not all that much...dying would be a
tiresome process...but nothing more...being
dead I didn't really mind at all.

EDMUND: Elizabeth!

ELIZABETH: Unless...unless there was nothing left. That
would make dying more than tiresome...it
would become a futile agony. All that effort...all
that sacrifice...all that...pain...of childbearing,
childrearing. The pain of loving you, Edmund
...and the pleasure. All that...becomes ridiculous, absurd, if all that's left is a heap of
radioactive ashes. I can't bear the thought of
that, Edmund.

EDMUND: You don't have to. It isn't going to happen.

ELIZABETH: I hope not. But I *had* to do my bit to try and
make sure it doesn't. Please understand,
Edmund, I didn't want to hurt you.

EDMUND: I know you didn't, you silly old thing. In any case, what's all this talk of dying...? You've years left yet. Time to sign dozens of those damn things.

ELIZABETH: ...No, Edmund...No...You have to know now ...it'll become obvious soon...

[EDMUND *looks at her. He steels himself.*]

EDMUND: ...How long?

ELIZABETH: Three months...at most. It could be sooner.

END OF ACT ONE

ACT TWO

The scene as at the end of Act One. Ten seconds have passed.

EDMUND: How long have you known?

ELIZABETH: Since the operation...they removed the uterus but...it wasn't fibroids...and it had already spread.

EDMUND: But why didn't they tell me?

ELIZABETH: I told them not to.

EDMUND: But why?

ELIZABETH: What was the point? What could you have done?

EDMUND: I...I could have supported you.

ELIZABETH: But you have...in the way you always have.

EDMUND: I needn't have gone down to the club so much.

ELIZABETH: Precisely.

EDMUND: ...That is cruel...

ELIZABETH: I don't mean it to be...What could you *do*? Really *do*? It has been far better for me to live out the rest of my life as normally as possible. To carry on the daily routine. After all, that is how we decided it was best to live, why should its imminent end change that? Life is hard enough without the need to charge every second with extra significance.

EDMUND: I should have *known*.

ELIZABETH: You've always hated long good-byes. How would you have coped with one lasting a year!

EDMUND: ...I would have liked the chance to show you.

ELIZABETH: ...Oh...Edmund...If I've misjudged you, I'm sorry.

[EDMUND *walks to the sideboard and pours another whisky.*]

EDMUND: ...Does Jerry know?

ELIZABETH: Oh please, Edmund...Don't torture both of us...

EDMUND: So he does.

ELIZABETH: ..Yes...

EDMUND: ...But he doesn't embarrass you by not being able to cope with...with difficult emotional situations.

ELIZABETH: He has been a great help. Mainly by ignoring the situation and just...gossiping over tea. I ignore his arthritis and tin leg, and he ignores my...my insides. And that is easy for him because he has never been acquainted with them. He has not lost an old friend. We have.

EDMUND: ...What will happen?

ELIZABETH: Nothing particularly dramatic...The pain will grow. I shall take more and more pills until...I suppose it'll be a toss up what gets me finally...the pills or...

EDMUND: In three months...

ELIZABETH: Or less.

EDMUND: What shall we do?

ELIZABETH: Just wait, Edmund. What else?

EDMUND: Do you want to...go away...go on holiday...see old friends?

ELIZABETH: No...I'm content to stay here...I'd rather stay here. Wherever I go I have to take it with me. It just doesn't seem worth it.

EDMUND: Do the children know?

ELIZABETH: No...

EDMUND: Do you mind if I invite them to the funeral?...I'm sorry...

ELIZABETH: Please don't be bitter, Edmund. I thought I
was doing the best thing...We have had a good
year...haven't we...? The children will have to
be told soon, of course, I do want to see them
before...well, before it becomes too painful for
us all.

EDMUND: And this is the way it ends?

[ELIZABETH *looks at him questioningly.*]

Our marriage, our life together...? Just peters
out like a guttering candle?

ELIZABETH: I have thought of blowing it out, but as long as
those pills control the pain, it didn't seem
worth it. In any case, I've had a good year.

EDMUND: I didn't mean that. Our life together. After fifty
odd years of marriage you're...you're leaving
and don't think it's important enough to men-
tion it...not to me anyway.

ELIZABETH: Oh Edmund...that's terrible. I didn't see it that
way at all.

EDMUND: What did Jerry think?

ELIZABETH: He thought...he thought I should tell you.

[EDMUND *nods.* ELIZABETH *involuntarily holds
her side.* EDMUND *notices.*]

EDMUND: Let's not go on. I don't want to make it...

ELIZABETH: Please, Edmund. I couldn't help holding my
side...I'm not asking for sympathy, to be treated like a child.

[EDMUND *looks at her.*]

That's how you think I've treated you?

[EDMUND *doesn't reply.*]

I'm sorry if I've given that impression. It
wasn't in my mind at all...I promise you.

EDMUND: Nevertheless...Oh, I don't want to go on with

this...leave me *some* dignity, my dear. You have told me now. Let it rest there.

ELIZABETH: Yes... but let me say I'm sorry. I *have* been selfish and I'm sorry.

[EDMUND *nods and takes a chair to sit near her. He takes her hands.*]

EDMUND: Well...it can't be long for my turn too...It isn't the end of the world, is it?

ELIZABETH: No...that's why I signed the petition. So it wouldn't be.

EDMUND: You never give up, do you?

[ELIZABETH *smiles and shakes her head.*]

Well, I don't want you to give up on that damned stitch there, whatever it is. Are you sure there's nothing anyone can do?

[ELIZABETH *nods.*]

We can bring up more reserves... get more opinions, go abroad...

ELIZABETH: I've seen the best men, Edmund. Old Jackson saw to that. Said you'd never forgive him if he hadn't done everything possible.

EDMUND: I'm not sure I shall forgive him in any case. He must have been part of your little conspiracy.

ELIZABETH: Under great protest.

EDMUND: Poor chap... I feel for him. He didn't stand a chance.

ELIZABETH: ...Has it been so hard, Edmund?

EDMUND: I'm not complaining...

ELIZABETH: But *has* it?

EDMUND: Yes. But then so is a day in the hunting field. I still used to enjoy it.

ELIZABETH: Oh! Really! What was I? The mare or the fox?

EDMUND: The whipper-in.

ELIZABETH: I didn't really spoil your career, did I?

EDMUND: I made full General. You can't have done that much harm.

ELIZABETH: But you were disappointed not to get your baton.

EDMUND: Who knows? I may not even have made Brigadier without you. I'm quite sure that Command must have realised that if I could cope with you, a brigade would be child's play.

ELIZABETH: Stop teasing, Edmund. I'm serious.

EDMUND: How else can I answer such damn silly questions? There has not been one day when I wished I'd married someone else.

ELIZABETH: There's still time.

EDMUND: If I've lasted fifty years, three months won't kill me...

[*They smile at each other.*]

ELIZABETH: ...But I'm not dead yet, Edmund. And I haven't finished what I want to do.

EDMUND: Then let's do it. Together...whatever it is...

ELIZABETH: I'm afraid you won't want to be with me when I do what I have to do.

[EDMUND *looks at her questioningly.*]

It's not enough just signing a piece of paper. I have to do more.

EDMUND: More of this Ban-the-Bomb thing?

ELIZABETH: Yes.

EDMUND: What *can* you do? You're in no state to go marching all over the country, or chaining yourself to the Greenham Common fence.

ELIZABETH: I hadn't thought of that!

EDMUND: So what is it you're planning to do?

ELIZABETH: In ten days, on Monday week, there's a big rally at the Albert Hall. I intend to speak at it.

EDMUND: Make a speech at a... a rally?

ELIZABETH: ...Yes...

EDMUND: And what will you say?

ELIZABETH: What I said to you just now, more or less.

EDMUND: You've been asked?

ELIZABETH: Yes.

EDMUND: ...I don't want to be cruel, Elizabeth...but don't you know why they've asked you?

ELIZABETH: Because I believe in the cause and they believe I could speak effectively, I suppose.

EDMUND: You're not as naive as that. You know you have been asked because you are Lady Elizabeth Milne, wife of General Milne.

ELIZABETH: Oh yes, of course! That goes without saying.

EDMUND: And you're prepared to let them use your name, *our* name?

ELIZABETH: Not them, *me*! I shall be using my name, our name. It didn't exactly harm your career that you were a Milne, son of Field Marshall Albert Milne. If names are important — and though I don't like it I have to admit they are — then let them be used sometimes for unselfish ends not just to ease a business deal or promote a career!

EDMUND: I don't think I deserve that.

ELIZABETH: You do if you keep on about *your* name. As if you leased it to me on conditions.

EDMUND: In an ideal marriage one doesn't have to state conditions. They are implied in a contract of love.

ELIZABETH: Honestly Edmund, sometimes you can be so...pompous, I half expect you will burst out laughing at yourself. But you never do.

EDMUND: Do you really want to quarrel now, not five minutes after you tell me...?

ELIZABETH: No...I don't...I don't...and I'm sorry; I have to allow for the shock... but... but...damn it all, Edmund, it is *me* that's dying!

> [*They look at each other.* ELIZABETH *breaks first and giggles.* EDMUND *joins her in a chuckle.*]

EDMUND: You know, Elizabeth, there must have been a hundred times in our marriage when I was convinced you'd drive me to an early grave...Oh my God, why is it all the metaphors suddenly seem wrong?

ELIZABETH: Do you know I've noticed that these last months: "I died laughing," "If looks could kill," "I'm dying to meet him"...on and on they go, as if all our lives we are trying to become familiar with death, but when it suddenly becomes a real familiar, all the moribund metaphors rise up and bite back — just to prove we've been fooling ourselves all along.

EDMUND: You've had the time to get used to it. You're going to have to give me some.

ELIZABETH: All I can spare.

EDMUND: And that doesn't include Monday week.

ELIZABETH: I'm afraid not...but don't worry, Edmund. After I've gone you can put it down to terminal madness or something.

> [EDMUND *looks at her a long time. He breaks and goes out of the room. He comes back with his hat and umbrella.*]

EDMUND: I need a walk, just a turn around the park...

ELIZABETH: Please don't leave me now.

EDMUND: Why? I thought that was what you wanted. Why you didn't tell me. To have me out of the way as much as possible.

ELIZABETH: You're angry about something...and I have enough to cope with — without your anger.

EDMUND: ...I cannot imagine why the company of a man for whom you have such contempt could be of any comfort.

ELIZABETH: Contempt?

EDMUND: Yes. Contempt. Suggesting I could put your actions down to "terminal madness"...Do you really believe that after you have gone I could possibly destroy something that was important to you, just to make myself more comfortable?

ELIZABETH: Oh...! I...I don't know what to say. 'Sorry' seems so weak...I was just fighting for my corner.

EDMUND: Fighting I understand. Possibly as well as you. I don't know how many men I have killed, or caused to be killed. But I respected them. The soldiers. I have never been cruel in war.

ELIZABETH: I'm sure you have always been an officer and a gentleman.

EDMUND: Even if you intend that as a sneer, I take it as a compliment.

ELIZABETH: A sneer? But I didn't.

[EDMUND *looks at her.*]

Or perhaps I did...Sometimes I think they're a contradiction in terms. How can you have a civilised war, kill in a gentlemanly fashion! It takes a man to come up with such a bizarre idea.

EDMUND: Perhaps it does. And I'm sure for you, therefore, it must be bizarre. But it means a lot to me.

ELIZABETH: I know. You remember that Rommel story you're always telling — where a Panzer unit caught a Long-Range Desert Group? And after his tanks had smashed through the ring of thin shelled vehicles killing most of the men — you see how attentive I've been; I remember all the technical terms — Rommel stepped out of the leading tank, walked up to the Commander, saluted him and said it was an honour to fight such a gallant enemy.

EDMUND: Yes.

ELIZABETH: I've never said so, but I find that a revolting story.

EDMUND: Why?

ELIZABETH: If I'd been Rommel I would probably have shot the Commander too. The only way I could have killed so many men would have been if I were so angry that I couldn't have just turned it off.

EDMUND: But Rommel wasn't angry. He was a soldier doing his duty.

ELIZABETH: Or a sportsman playing just another game. But the counters were sons, husbands, lovers...

EDMUND: Then it's probably a good thing that the bomb is in the hands of professional soldiers. When you and I are fighting side by side on Dover beach you'd probably be so angry you'd throw the thing just to wipe out a single landing craft.

ELIZABETH: Oh yes! I probably would! I don't trust me any more than I trust you. It's why you don't like playing bridge with me — "You always take it so personally," you say. Well it's true — I do. So I don't play the stupid game.

EDMUND: But you don't always have a choice as to whether to go to war or not. Stalin tried everything he knew to avoid a war with Hitler but he had to fight in the end. Or submit.

ELIZABETH: I'm glad he fought. It saved *our* neck. Edmund, I'm not particularly proud of the human race — or even European civilisation as it's called. Actually I've more sympathy with the cannibal whose chief objection to the Second World War was that it was such a waste of meat.

EDMUND: Oh!

ELIZABETH: At least that's practical...and with those ideas he wouldn't have bombed Hiroshima — or Dresden... I know there may be a war; it seems that we're too stupid, greedy or whatever to stop playing these games. All I want to do is to remove the Armageddon counter. If we can do that at least our children will be free to make the same stupid choices we have. Or perhaps... perhaps...they might even make better ones.

EDMUND: If Ivan's running the country, our children won't be free to make *any* choices.

ELIZABETH: Or grandchildren, or great, great, great grandchildren. Someone in the future. The important thing is that there will be a future.

EDMUND: ...There is something...appalling that we should be discussing politics at a time like this.

ELIZABETH: Oh, there isn't! What should we be talking about? What sort of flowers I want? I'm still alive, Edmund.

EDMUND: I can see that! It's me that feels that someone has dropped an H-bomb. Within five minutes I hear...that...you're terminally ill...and learn that you didn't trust me enough to tell me...and on top of that for the first time understand with

what contempt you hold all the values upon
which I've built my life.

ELIZABETH: That's not true.

EDMUND: It is! You have so little regard for the whole
way I've spent my life, you'd have more respect
for me if I knocked off our neighbours in order
to cook them for Sunday lunch.

[ELIZABETH *laughs*.]

ELIZABETH: Oh, Edmund!

EDMUND: On second thoughts they can have a week's
reprieve — we'll eat Jerry on Sunday.

ELIZABETH: Now I know why we've lasted. Why I love you.
I know you hate it, Edmund, but you do have a
sense of humour.

EDMUND: Why should I hate it?

ELIZABETH: It's very subversive. Before you can laugh you
have to see both points of view.

EDMUND: I have never doubted the values of the Army.

ELIZABETH: No.

EDMUND: Or felt I was playing a game when I was defending our way of life.

ELIZABETH: No.

EDMUND: Or believed that the defence of that way of life
entailed the lowering of standards of conduct
towards the enemy.

ELIZABETH: No.

EDMUND: ...Or doubted for one moment that I loved you.

ELIZABETH: ...No.

EDMUND: ...Even when you were having an affair with
Rawlings.

[*A long pause.*]

ELIZABETH: ...You *did* know, then...?

EDMUND: Of course...

ELIZABETH: How?

EDMUND: The Army only looks big from the outside. It's a small club really.

ELIZABETH: You never said anything...all these years...

[EDMUND *shrugs.*]

So why now...?

EDMUND: ...When you draw up a peace treaty it's as well to clear up all outstanding issues.

ELIZABETH: A peace treaty?

EDMUND: I'd like that...for these last months...wouldn't you?

ELIZABETH: Of course. Not that I'm aware we've been at war.

EDMUND: There's all sorts of wars. Hot. Cold. Phony ...and the worst, luke-warm. Just sporadic sniping. Random casualties and no solution.

ELIZABETH: What do you want to know about Peter?

EDMUND: Nothing. I know when it started. I know when it ended. The part in the middle I can imagine — all too clearly.

ELIZABETH: I'm sorry. Really very sorry.

EDMUND: There's no need to say any more. Just so that it's out in the open.

ELIZABETH: You must have been terribly hurt.

EDMUND: Just one of the random casualties. I got over it.

ELIZABETH: ...And what about you? Did you ever...?

EDMUND: Break my vows? No. Never felt the need.

ELIZABETH: *That's* hard to believe. But anyway, you always behaved as an officer and a gentleman.

EDMUND: I'm not ashamed of it.

ELIZABETH: You should be proud of it. When Peter cut and run even I began to appreciate those values.

EDMUND: You can't expect a man to behave as a gentleman in a situation where a gentleman would never be.

ELIZABETH: Oh, Edmund! What a strange black and white world you inhabit.

EDMUND: Old-fashioned, isn't it!

ELIZABETH: Yes, it is. But in some ways very attractive.

EDMUND: But not in all ways — in your opinion.

ELIZABETH: No, because the world isn't black and white. It's grey and bloody and... confusing.

EDMUND: Elizabeth, I am perfectly aware that I'm a black and white dinosaur in a technicolour world. I am also aware that the dinosaurs became extinct *because* they couldn't adapt to the new world. I am not completely blind.

ELIZABETH: I never thought you were. But don't despair, Edmund, after the bomb drops the world may become fit for dinosaurs again.

EDMUND: I don't want to survive that. If it *is* ever dropped, it's failed to achieve its aim. But I don't believe it will.

ELIZABETH: Such faith! It's charming but doomed. When we were married you had the same faith that I would remain a faithful wife. I didn't.

EDMUND: But I didn't drop the bomb.

ELIZABETH: No. You pretended it hadn't happened.

EDMUND: I didn't!

ELIZABETH: You *acted* as though it hadn't happened. Perhaps that's the hope. If the Russians take West Germany or France we may just act as though they haven't.

EDMUND: It happened before — when Hitler took Austria and Czechoslovakia and the Rhineland. And that's why I hate your damned Ban-the-Bombers. They make a war more likely by convincing the Communists we might do the same again

and some Neil Kinnock or other* will fly into
Heathrow with a rolled umbrella waving a
piece of paper, saying, 'Peace in our Time'.

ELIZABETH: I don't think Mr. Kinnock* would be very
pleased to be compared with Neville Chamber-
lain.

EDMUND: But don't you see, Elizabeth, that the bomb has
worked? We've had peace in Europe for forty
years.

ELIZABETH: In 1945 we'd have been shocked if we'd known
that that would have been a cause for surprise
or self-congratulation.

EDMUND: I wouldn't have been.

ELIZABETH: No. But you're a soldier, dedicated to war.

EDMUND: To peace. To winning it; then keeping it.

ELIZABETH: But you're only really happy when you're doing
the winning bit.

EDMUND: Because I'm a practical man, Elizabeth. You
call me arrogant, but it's you that believe you
can change human nature. The world is full of
conflicting interests. You're right, there *is* greed
and selfishness and naked ambition rampant
all over the globe. I don't pretend I can change
all that; all I can do is defend my corner, keep
our little space free so that our children can
have the same chances we had to make — or
break — our lives. And damn it all, it's worked.
The bomb *is* a defence.

ELIZABETH: ...We won't agree on this, Edmund.

EDMUND: No.

---

*U.S. text: ...some British Prime Minister or other...
I don't think Mrs. Thatcher...

ELIZABETH: Are there any other terms for your peace
treaty?

EDMUND: I want assurances that from now on you won't
attempt to hide anything from me.

ELIZABETH: I promise you, if Peter Rawlings comes back
you'll be the first one to know.

EDMUND: That would shock us all — especially his wife.
He died eighteen months ago.

ELIZABETH: Really...? I didn't know...I thought they went
out to South Africa.

EDMUND: He did...to his son's.

ELIZABETH: So how did you know?

EDMUND: I made it my business to find out where he was
— what he was up to.

ELIZABETH: You dark horse!

EDMUND: I permitted myself an extra large scotch the day
I heard he'd died. I'd outlived the bugger! And
when I came home we made love. It was
wonderful.

ELIZABETH: Eighteen months ago...I remember that night
...it was one of the last times...I've often
thought of it...It *was* wonderful... So, that was
Peter's last gift, was it? A marvellous night with
my husband.

EDMUND: You could put it like that.

ELIZABETH: I thought you were delighting in me, not danc-
ing on Peter's grave.

EDMUND: Oh, I was... the other merely added piquancy.

ELIZABETH: I'm not sure that doesn't constitute crowing
over a defeated enemy, which is definitely conduct unbecoming.

EDMUND: Guilty.

[*They laugh. A slight discomfort makes* ELIZ-
ABETH *hold her side again.*]

...All right, old girl?

ELIZABETH: Yes!

EDMUND: Would you like a pill...?

ELIZABETH: No, it's too soon...but you might refill this. [*She holds up her glass.*] Cirrhosis of the liver has lost all its terrors.

EDMUND: Right...

[*He takes the glass.*]

ELIZABETH: But I think I'll make that one of *my* conditions of the peace treaty.

EDMUND: What?

ELIZABETH: That I am allowed to hold my side without you jumping all over the place like a cat on hot bricks.

EDMUND: Agreed.

ELIZABETH: And there's a harder condition.

EDMUND: What's that?

ELIZABETH: That as far as possible, for as long as possible, we carry on our lives just as we have for the last...twenty years.

EDMUND: That's difficult.

ELIZABETH: I know. But I do want it. Very much.

EDMUND: I've been out such a lot, the club and...

ELIZABETH: I know, I know. That's what I wanted, and it's what I still want.

EDMUND: You ask an awful lot.

ELIZABETH: I know.

EDMUND: ...Very well...

ELIZABETH: Thank you.

[EDMUND *returns to her and hands her the glass. He has refilled his.*]

EDMUND: Cheers.

ELIZABETH: Cheers.

[*They drink.*]

We'd *better* get back to normal as soon as possible. [*She indicates her glass.*] If we go on like this, we'll both be dead by the end of the week!

EDMUND: ...Do you *have* to go on with this speech thing?

ELIZABETH: Yes.

EDMUND: That's not "carrying on our lives as we have for twenty years."

ELIZABETH: ...No...but it is in a way.

EDMUND: Hardly. I think I would have noticed if you'd taken up a political career.

ELIZABETH: Do you think I haven't thought and...worried...and wanted to do something?

EDMUND: You haven't said anything...

ELIZABETH: You haven't said anything about a lot of things. Does that mean you haven't been thinking about them?

EDMUND: I try to be positive. Not worry about things I can do nothing about.

ELIZABETH: ...Then you'll be able to cope with this little situation.

> [*She pats her abdomen and returns to her drink.* EDMUND *sags as the realisation of* ELIZABETH'*s condition sinks into him.* ELIZABETH *isn't looking.*]

EDMUND: ...Betty!

ELIZABETH: Betty...! You haven't called me Betty since... Edmund, what's the matter?

EDMUND: Betty... Betty...

ELIZABETH: Edmund!

EDMUND: I'm... sorry... sorry... Here we are...arguing... about...about a...damned...silly speech and you...you...

ELIZABETH: Oh...sit down, Edmund... Here...come on...

[*She sits* EDMUND *in a chair. By now he is crying.*]

Oh, Edmund... I need you to be strong... as you always have been...I know it's difficult...

EDMUND: Difficult...! We have to do something...We can't just sit here and wait...

ELIZABETH: ...There isn't anything to do...Let me get Jackson here. He'll explain to you...and maybe give you something.

EDMUND: What's the good of sending for a man who's already admitted defeat...? We have to find somebody else.

ELIZABETH: I've seen the best. You must believe that...I can't go through it all again. All the prodding and...oh, the indignity of it all. And it isn't admitting defeat, Edmund. I've had my three score years and ten — and a little bonus. Just because you're having a bigger bonus mustn't make me greedy!

EDMUND: I've always thought...that it would be me... that...

ELIZABETH: Yes...so have I, but it's me that's the lucky one. I'm sorry, Edmund.

EDMUND: No. It's me that should be sorry...blubbering away like a...like...

ELIZABETH: Like a man who loves his wife. To be quite honest, I think I'd have been a bit put out if my news hadn't had *some* reaction.

EDMUND: No, no... You've a right to expect...support ...not collapse...

[*He pulls himself together.*]

I'm sorry. It won't happen again.

ELIZABETH: Oh, Edmund...Why must you ask so much of

yourself — no...so little really.

EDMUND: What are you talking about?

ELIZABETH: ...Your wife tells you that she is...is going to die shortly, and you feel it's some terrible moral failure that you cry about it...Your wife has an affair lasting...what was it, two years, and you...

EDMUND: Two years and thirteen days...

> [ELIZABETH *looks at him. A long pause. She goes back to her seat.*]

ELIZABETH: ...We have lived on different planets.

EDMUND: And what did you expect me to do about it? Have scenes, rows, throw you out, call out Rawlings for a duel? What did you expect?

ELIZABETH: ...I don't know.

EDMUND: I can't believe that. You know damn well. You knew you were safe if you avoided open scandal.

ELIZABETH: Did I...? Perhaps I did...

EDMUND: Of course you knew...You'd go off for those weekends...painting, you said...water colours ...we still have one of your alibis hanging on the walls. Look at it... "Sunset over Lulworth Cove." How did you manage to find the time...?

> [*He tears the painting off the wall and hurls it across the room.*]

...Or did you paint it secretly at home so that you wouldn't have to waste good rutting time!

ELIZABETH: Oh, my God!

EDMUND: Lying sweating under that...apology for a man... having him inside you...that weak... effeminate... He couldn't control his battalion any more than he could control himself...

ELIZABETH: I assure you he wasn't effeminate.

EDMUND: Oh, that's your definition of a man, is it? Just a stiff prick...?

ELIZABETH: Edmund!

EDMUND: Providing he can get it up he's a man? Well, I tell you there's a lot more to a man than that! It's to do with control...self-respect...

ELIZABETH: *Mens sana in corpore sano...*

EDMUND: Yes! Bloody yes! A healthy mind in a healthy body. It's true. Look at you! Look at you now. What went wrong finally? Eh? What was it that finally gave way. Your cunt!

[*He storms over to the whisky.*]

ELIZABETH: No, Edmund. Please don't drink any more.

[EDMUND *ignores her and continues making his drink.*]

...How have you managed to keep this inside you all these years!

EDMUND: What else should I have done?

ELIZABETH: And why now? If you wanted to clear it up, why wait until it's too late?

EDMUND: I told you...

ELIZABETH: To make a peace treaty! Oh my God, Edmund. Grow up! What do you want to me to do? Cross my legs and call "Pax"...? You talk about a healthy mind in a healthy body — what about *your* mind! The only time in our entire life that you can bring yourself to give a proper name to my vagina instead of some coy euphemism is when you're half drunk and half mad with self-pity.

EDMUND: Self-pity!

ELIZABETH: Yes! What do you think all this is about! I'm

going to die and you're going to be left...to your
club, your bridge, your...empty friends, fighting old wars, winning at Dunkirk.

EDMUND: You'd think more of me, I suppose, if I was
sneaking off with some whore.

ELIZABETH: ...As Peter sneaked off with his?

[EDMUND *subsides into his chair.*]

EDMUND: I'm sorry... I deserved that...I don't know
what's come over me... I do, of course...delayed
shock... Seen it often enough in the men...
after being under fire... Said the most out-
rageous things, some of them... I had to learn to
cultivate deafness.

ELIZABETH: I could do that, but I won't. I'm glad I heard
your heart speak, unfiltered.

EDMUND: I hope you made the most of it. It won't happen
again.

ELIZABETH: Then we'll both be the losers.

EDMUND: It's too late to change now. "Let it all hang
out", as they say, I understand. The experience
is as distressing as the expression.

ELIZABETH: Do you want to talk about it? Really have me
tell you exactly what happened?

EDMUND: No.

ELIZABETH: I wish you would. I assure you it was not as
sordid as you believe it to be.

EDMUND: How can it be other? It was deceitful, underhand... sly.

ELIZABETH: It's true I didn't tell you...and tried to save you
embarrassment...

EDMUND: And if he hadn't "cut and run", how would it
have ended? If he'd been so besotted as to
dump Jane and *his* kids, if he'd asked you to

run away with him, would you have still continued to "save me embarrassment"?

ELIZABETH: I suppose I knew really that it would never come to that.

EDMUND: So you knew it would always be hole in the corner — if you'll pardon the expression.

ELIZABETH: Beggars can't be choosers.

EDMUND: Was I so inadequate?

ELIZABETH: Oh, Edmund...Can't you see? The fact that we are having this conversation after...what...? thirty years, means... Oh, it's grotesque... You've kept this buried, festering all this time. And I suppose if I hadn't signed that petition it never would have come out.

EDMUND: But why did you *have* to... with *him*?

ELIZABETH: ...Well... I...

EDMUND: I don't want to know.
    [*A long pause.*]
    I'm sorry... It was stupid to bring it up. Especially now... bad show.
    [*He gets up and goes to get the picture. It is broken.*]
    I'm sorry about this, too...I'll get it mended...

ELIZABETH: Throw it away. Do you think I'd put it back now?

EDMUND: Of course you can. I'll...

ELIZABETH: In the basket... please!
    [EDMUND *hesitates, then places the picture in the waste-paper basket.*]

EDMUND: Anyway, I'm sorry...

ELIZABETH: It doesn't matter...Edmund. I've always loved you — after my fashion. Our marriage wasn't perfect. But whose is? I've respected you and I wouldn't have willingly hurt you... I'm not saying the affair with Peter was unimportant. It was very important to me.

EDMUND: Please!

ELIZABETH: No. I've got to go on. I won't go into details. It was a fling — wild, I suppose. But I absolutely needed it. Just for once in my life I had to...to act...just act. Abandon the rules of the game we'd always played. It was painful... especially at the end...but absolutely necessary. I don't know if all life can be lived at that pitch of intensity. Probably not. But if I'd never once felt that...feeling. Never once taken that step into the dark — or into that blinding light, I would feel now I'd never really lived at all. I wouldn't have understood things in the way I do.

EDMUND: What things?

ELIZABETH: You for a start...and war.

EDMUND: Me?

ELIZABETH: Yes...You left me to go to your mistress, the smoke, the blood, the excitement. That was your step into the blinding light. And if you think I wasn't jealous, you're wrong!

EDMUND: How can you compare one's duty with...?

ELIZABETH: Duty? That just makes you luckier. Your orgasm won you the M.C. and D.S.O., mine a private hell.

EDMUND: So that's what you're doing now, is it? With this petition and speeches? Having another fling.

ELIZABETH: No...! How little you understand me, Edmund. I hate it. Can't you imagine what it's been like waiting for the petition to be published? Knowing how upset you were going to be?

EDMUND: I find it very hard to imagine your having any fears concerning *my* reaction.

ELIZABETH: I wasn't frightened...just...weary. This isn't exciting for me, a substitute climax. This really is "One doing one's duty."

EDMUND: Damned queer idea of duty.

ELIZABETH: Is it? Not for me. I'm convinced I'm right to be worried about another war, that our policies make it more likely. And it's my duty to try to change that.

EDMUND: Your premise is wrong. It doesn't make war more likely.

ELIZABETH: Even if you *are* right, it doesn't alter my position. I agree with you it may be better to be dead than red. But try out the slogan, "Better two-headed children than red."

[EDMUND *shakes his head.*]

Let's not quarrel any more about it...Please...I have to go on with the speech. If you prefer, I'll move out, take a room somewhere...

EDMUND: Don't be so damn silly. If we survived the Rawlings affair, this is trivial by comparison.

ELIZABETH: Is it...? Is it really...? What strange values!

EDMUND: Not to me.

ELIZABETH: No...

EDMUND: Of course it's trivial. How can I take it seriously? You describe it as duty. In which case it has always been your duty. Is duty something that just pops up in the last five minutes of life, like remembering to put the cat out before you go to bed?

ELIZABETH: I should have been campaigning for years...? Since '45?

EDMUND: If that was your *duty*.

ELIZABETH: And how would you have taken that!

EDMUND: I don't know. But if I'd have been convinced you were doing what you had to do, I suppose I would have coped somehow.

ELIZABETH: That's easy to say now. Look at your reaction to that petition which can't affect your career at this late stage. My God, I can imagine what you'd have said if I'd marched to Aldermaston in '59.

EDMUND: That isn't the point. Maybe we *would* have split up. I don't know. I'm just explaining why I don't take your petition particularly seriously. You say you've been this armchair secret socialist all these years. Well, what does it matter! One Labour vote from Belgravia isn't going to shake the citadels of capitalism. At least with Rawlings you *did* get into bed with him. That's why I take it more seriously.

ELIZABETH: Yes... you're right. I've been a coward...A deserter in the face of the enemy.

EDMUND: Whatever you think, I've never been that.

ELIZABETH: No... it's unfair to blame my weakness on you. I have to take the responsibility for myself. If I haven't been open with you it's because I suppose I was having it both ways. Running with the hounds and secretly hoping the fox would escape. It's not very attractive, I know, but it doesn't alter my conviction that I have to do what I can *now*... You've always said it's the last battle that counts.

[*A long pause.*]

EDMUND: Shall I get us some fresh coffee?

ELIZABETH: There isn't time.

EDMUND: Time...?

ELIZABETH: It's Wednesday. Bridge day, remember? Lunch at the club and...

EDMUND: Surely you don't expect me to carry on with...?

ELIZABETH: You promised. Remember? Our treaty?

EDMUND: But...

ELIZABETH: No buts. We have to go on.

EDMUND: ...And Jerry. Is he coming around for tea?

ELIZABETH: Yes.

EDMUND: How can I play bridge when I'll be thinking...?

ELIZABETH: Just as you carried on, when I was carrying on with Peter. Only this time all you have to imagine is two old fogies gossiping over tea and scones.

EDMUND: Very well.

ELIZABETH: Thank you. It's the whole point, you see, Edmund. The carrying on. Me. You. Us. The world. I feel I'm on a rocket zooming away. The world looks smaller and smaller — and infinitely more precious — just like those marvellous pictures from the moon. A perfect jewel. If I'd been one of those spacemen I know I would have loved it, the earth, home. Of course I'm not like them, I'm not coming back, but that only makes it more precious, not less. When it fades out of sight I *have* to know that my time on it didn't spoil it. I don't want to look back and see some great flaw appear, then another and another until it cracks and splinters, or disappears behind a poisonous cloud.

EDMUND: You're a tough old soldier, aren't you?

ELIZABETH: I had a tough old drill sergeant, didn't I?

EDMUND: Hm...

[*He looks around for his hat and umbrella. He goes to retrieve them and walks to the door.*]

...Give my regards to Jerry. Tell him I think he's a bloody fool to have signed that petition... and that I'm...I'm grateful for the support he's given you in the past year...

[ELIZABETH *goes to him.*]

ELIZABETH: Oh...Eddy...Eddy...that is conduct...most becoming.

[*She kisses him.* EDMUND *goes out.* ELIZABETH *looks around the room. She goes to the waste-paper basket and retrieves the picture. She returns to her chair and smooths the picture out on her knees. She smiles and tears it slowly in half.*]

THE END

Brian Clark   WHOSE LIFE IS IT ANYWAY?

The play that launched Brian Clark to fame in 1978 when it transferred from the Mermaid to the Savoy Theatre en route for smash-hit success on Broadway. The central character is faced with a future of total dependence on a life-support machine. In his fight to determine the course of his own life – and death – he encounters fierce opposition from the medical profession.

Brian Clark   CAN YOU HEAR ME AT THE BACK?

Brian Clark's second West-End stage play, where he turns his attention to the world of architects and town planners who, instead of designing buildings that fit the human scale, seem only to succeed in creating a succession of 'people filing cabinets'.

Ronald Harwood   THE DRESSER

Michael Billington found *The Dresser* '...a wonderfully affectionate and intelligent play about the theatre. It captures not only the equivocal relationship between star and dresser, it also conveys the bitchiness, the sentiment, the anecdotage, plus the feeling that the backstage world is itself a little kingdom, a tatty Camelot worshipping a prop Holy Grail.' Released as a feature film in 1984, starring Albert Finney and Tom Courtenay.

Ronald Harwood   TRAMWAY ROAD

Set in Cape Town in 1951, one year after the Population Registration Act was passed in South Africa. In the 1950s Tramway Road was a notorious Cape Coloured ghetto located within the predominantly white residential suburb of Sea Point. Ronald Harwood explores the influence that Tramway Road exerts over four characters: an expatriate English couple, Arthur and Dora Langley; Emil, a young man with dreams of becoming an actor in London; and Jacob, a house servant.

Julian Mitchell   ANOTHER COUNTRY

One of the West End's resounding successes of 1982, winning the SWET award for 'Play of the Year'. The setting is an English public school in the 1930's. The two central characters, Guy Bennett and Tommy Judd, are both, in their own different ways, rebels and outsiders who dare to fight against the system.

Julian Mitchell   FRANCIS

Francis of Assisi was a man totally dedicated to a missionary life of poverty and simplicity. He wished to follow the gospels literally and to be a true disciple of Christ. In this play Julian Mitchell writes about the forces that turned Brother Francis into Saint Francis.

Brian Thompson   TURNING OVER

A deliciously funny satire on how television documentaries are made. A BBC film crew is on a hill station in India, making a programme for a series entitled 'I could be happy here'. But the presenter, director and technicians are far from happy as they battle with the climate, the food and the souring relationships.

Hugh Whitemore   PACK OF LIES

Based on the real events surrounding an American couple living in Britain, Helen and Peter Kroger, who were found guilty of spying for the Russians in 1961. The action centres around the Jackson family who as friends and neighbours of the Krogers are drawn into a conspiracy of betrayal.

For a complete catalogue of our plays write or telephone:
Amber Lane Press, 9 Middle Way, Oxford OX2 7LH.
Tel. Oxford 50545